THE RELATIONSHIP DICTIONARY

THE RELATIONSHIP DICTIONARY

MATTIAS GORANSSON

THE OVERLOOK PRESS
WOODSTOCK • NEW YORK

First published in the United States in 2000 by
The Overlook Press, Peter Mayer Publishers, Inc.
Lewis Hollow Road
Woodstock, New York 12498

Cataloging-in-Publication Data is available from the Library of Congress

Manufactured in the United States of America
First Edition
1 3 5 7 9 8 6 4 2
ISBN 1-58567-005-7

THE RELATIONSHIP DICTIONARY

THE RELATIONSHIP DICTIONARY

Introduction

I. Vocabulary
The Relationship Dictionary defines phenomena and concepts overlooked by other linguistic sources. As a result, many of the terms defined here may seem alien even to those with highly developed vocabularies. To facilitate understanding, the terms are created, as much as possible, by the joining of semantic units that should be somewhat familiar to English language speakers.

II. Definitions
The term is the word (or phrase) in bold face. It is followed by a concise definition. The text which follows each of the definitions is intended mainly as a key to a more profound understanding of the mechanics of the terms that *The Relationship Dictionary* is attempting to elucidate.

III. Colloquialisms and Slang
The Relationship Dictionary makes no claim to adhere to Standard English. Due to the particular linguistic terrain addressed by *The Relationship Dictionary*, colloquial and slang language appear frequently. The publisher advises people with a puritanical stance towards the English language not to read any further.

IV. Proper Nouns
Concerning the use of proper names: All names used in the dictionary are, according to the author, fictitious. We kindly ask that you please refrain from sending us complaints or questions regarding this matter.

The Bullshitting Privilege

THE DISCREPANCY BETWEEN THE THINGS A WOMAN WILL ALLOW HERSELF TO SAY PUBLICLY ABOUT HER PARTNER AND WHAT SHE WILL ALLOW HIM TO SAY ABOUT HER.

John didn't mean to spy, it was just that nobody seemed to have heard him when he came back to get the car keys. Laura and her girlfriends were talking and laughing in the kitchen. He could hear them from the stairwell.

"You should have seen Fred's face when I told him about the crabs."

There was a round of laughs all around.

"Mark still grunts like a pig when he comes."

Another one.

John had thought he might peep in one more time before finally leaving and give Laura a kiss, but he changed his mind. He stood there in the dark stairwell listening.

"If Brad didn't wax his shoulders, he would literally be as hairy as an ape."

What were they doing in there, recording a laugh track? Suddenly another female voice was heard.

"You should see all the pimples on Tommy's ass."

"He he he."

A very large lump started to form in John's stomach. What the hell were they up to?

Soon he heard a voice he recognized far too well.

"John still has terrible hang-ups about the size of his cute little dick."

"Is it still as crooked as it was when you first started going out?"

"No—it's gotten worse!"

"He he he, ho ho ho, ha ha ha."

Suddenly he heard a chair scraping against the floor. One of the girls was going to the bathroom. Quick as a flash, John slipped out of the apartment. Without a sound, he pulled the door shut.

He stood on the landing for a few minutes to catch his breath. Then he ran to the car.

In the car, he threw on a Henry Rollins tape that was hidden in the back of the glove compartment. He put it on and turned up the volume until the speakers almost burst. He beat his knuckles on the dashboard to the music like some deranged pop star. At The Sporting Life sports bar he sat down in the midst of his friends. All the guys were there. Beer, peanuts and the lovely face of the sports commentator all over the giant television screen. A little later Fred asked casually, "How are things going for you and Laura nowadays?"

"All right. The same as always," John said. "How do you think the Yankees are going to do this season?"

Catastrophist

A (USUALLY FEMALE) PARTNER IN A RELATIONSHIP WHO—BECAUSE THE RELATIONSHIP HAS ACHIEVED A CERTAIN LEVEL OF PEACE AND TRANQUILLITY—FEELS BETTER THE WORSE THINGS ARE.

Bill looked at the red blanket laying carelessly on the couch. He was bewildered. Hadn't he just folded it up neatly? And the issues of *Wallpaper** which lay scattered on the coffee table, hadn't they been neatly stacked on the bookshelf not a moment ago? The doorbell rang.

"Can you answer the door, honey. I'm fixing my hair," Pamela shouted from the bathroom.

Strange, Bill thought. *Didn't she fix her hair an hour ago?* He opened the door for Morgan and Chelsea. A second later, Pamela came running from the bathroom with a towel around her head.

"Oh, my God. I'm late as always. And the whole apartment is a mess. Bill, can't you pick up a few things in the living room? The magazines are spread out all over the coffee table and that blanket needs to be folded and . . . Please, come on in," she said pushing Bill towards the mess.

Their guests took off their coats. Bill went into the living room without saying anything. Suddenly, Pamela let out a small scream.

"The tonic! We're out of tonic. We need tonic for the drinks."

"But when we were shopping . . ." Bill said, but Pamela cut him off.

"Honey, would you mind running down to the corner and getting some tonic?" she whined.

Bill tied his shoes with a sigh. He was positive that he had put two bottles of tonic in their cart at the supermarket. In the back of his head he thought to himself that Pamela must have put them back on the shelf. Sometimes he didn't understand anything at all.

Five minutes later he came back with two bottles of tonic. Pamela was telling their guests about her problems with the new home gym.

"But you knew it was pure trash even before you got it," Bill suddenly blurted out. "Sandra had ordered one just like it, and she told you that hers broke down after her first session."

Pamela didn't say anything. She only gave him that cold, hard gaze that she gave him when he had said something really, really stupid

"I heard that you found an afford-
able one-bedroom apartment with
a view of Central Park."

"Yeah, but there's
no balcony."

Chameleon Recoil

THE REACTION ONE IS LIABLE TO EXPERIENCE WHEN THE SYM-
BIOSIS IN A RELATIONSHIP HAS GONE PERHAPS A BIT FURTHER
THAN IT SHOULD HAVE.

Linda stared at Paul. He was sunk deep in their mossy green couch from Pottery Barn reading the latest issue of *Wallpaper**. Something was wrong. Was it the thick plastic frames on his glasses or the dark brown turtleneck?

Ever since that day in January when she and Paul ran into his old friends Frank and Billy from New Jersey, these thoughts descended upon her with greater and greater frequency.

Paul had politely declined his old friend's invitation to a Van Halen reunion gig. He had explained that he had already committed to a guest DJing spot at The Tunnel. That evening Linda lay in bed pondering what Paul had been like when they had first met. She remembered how impressed she had been by his care-free, down-to-earth attitude.

At the time, Linda had been dreaming about moving to London to study industrial design. Paul had been talking about breeding Burmese Mountain dogs in Vermont. Once, during an office party at the ad agency she worked for, Paul had missed a reference to the architect Louis Sullivan, launching into his early childhood memories of The Ed Sullivan Show. She remembered that she had stood there feeling both incredibly attracted to and repulsed by him at the same time.

"Why don't you shave off that ridiculous goatee? It just doesn't suit you," Linda hissed. Paul looked up innocently from the depths of their preciously purchased couch.

"What?"

"And put down that damn magazine. What do you know about what's hip?"

"But the goatee was your idea. And this is your magazine."

Linda didn't say anything. She just sat there, suddenly paralyzed. When her eyes again came into focus she found herself staring at her left shirt sleeve. Dark brown. Turtleneck. She tore her gaze away from her sleeve and caught her reflection in the Sony TV set in the corner of the room. Glasses with thick plastic frames. Screaming, she ran out of the room.

Peter shook his head, pulled their mustard color cashmere throw up over his legs and again immersed himself in the extremely interesting article on reinforced concrete in the Polish aesthetic that he had been reading.

The Chip-Scarfing Phase

THAT PERIOD IN A RELATIONSHIP WHEN IT BECOMES APPARENT THAT GETTING REALLY CLOSE TO SOMEBODY IS NOT ALWAYS THE BEAUTIFUL THING ONE THOUGHT IT WOULD BE.

Anna felt her stomach gurgling. They probably should have stopped at one bag of chips. But John had insisted on sour cream and onion and she wanted barbecue so they'd bought two.

"Pass me the chocolate pudding," John said.

"I seem to have finished it," Anna answered.

"I'll go and get the cheese cake."

John stood up slowly, scratched his butt and slouched towards the fridge. Anna felt the need to fart. The question was how long John was going to stay in the kitchen. She was so comfortable lying in front of the TV that she didn't want to get up. She tried to let it out without a sound. Just at that moment, John came back.

Anna pretended to be engrossed in the movie. The stink lay heavy in the room.

John didn't say anything but looked very uncomfortable. Finally, Anna couldn't keep quiet any longer.

"I'm sorry. I think I farted."

"You too?" John said.

Suddenly, he didn't look uncomfortable at all. With a loud clap he let out another fart. Anna couldn't help giggling.

What if she had been able to see into the future? What if only six months ago—when she and John still cleaned the apartment, cooked and locked the bathroom door—she had been able to see how they would be living today? Two couch potatoes in sweat-suits, hungover in front of the VCR, with a bag of chips each.

John belched. Anna took a nail file and started filing down a callous on her heel.

"You haven't shaved your legs in a long time," John commented.

"Oh, I seem to have stopped doing that," Anna said.

"Good, then you'll leave my disposable razors alone," John said.

Commitment Phobia

A YOUNG MAN'S ALMOST PATHOLOGICAL AVERSION TO ACKNOWL-
EDGING THE POSSIBILITY OF PERMANENCE IN A RELATIONSHIP.

Matt and Tom ran into each other on the 1/9 train in the evening on their way home from work. Matt glanced at the little gift box in Tom's hands. Even with his own very shabby track record for pleasing and holding on to women—or maybe precisely because of it—Tom was quite familiar with the particular shade of blue of the Tiffany's gift box. "Are you and Mona getting engaged?" he asked.

"You're kidding, right?" Tom answered.

"I thought that might be an engagement ring."

"This is just a pair of earrings. Engaged . . .if you only knew how far from the realm of possibility that is," Tom laughed a forced laugh.

"But you've lived together for four years."

"Yeah, but you know how expensive it is to live here. When Mona broke up with her old boyfriend, she couldn't afford a place of her own. Just about the same time my roommate moved to California. Living together was the most practical solution."

That night Tom lay next to Mona in their king-sized bed, both of them soaked with sweat. It had been a perfect night. Good food, great booze and terrific sex.

Mona had been so happy when he gave her the earrings. She seemed to have forgotten how angry she'd been in the morning before work when Tom announced he wouldn't be joining her at her parents' for Christmas.

Tom let his gaze wander over her, and a warm feeling surged up from deep inside him. It was overwhelming. They really had a good thing going after all. She was such a special woman.

"Mona . . ." Tom said.

"Yes, what is it?" Mona asked.

"There's something I want to ask you."

"Yes?"

"Something I've been wanting to ask you for a long time now."

"Yes . . .?"

"I . . . well . . . Never mind." Tom simply could not remember what it was he had thought to ask Mona only seconds before.

"I found a Be Sure pregnancy test in Mona's bag."

"Maybe it's time we quit our jobs and took that long trip to Thailand we've been talking about."

Conveyor Belt Shock

THE STATE OF PROFOUND CONFUSION THAT ARISES WHEN ONE'S REPLACEMENT IN A RELATIONSHIP HAS BOOTED YOU OFF THE CONVEYOR BELT OF YOUR EX'S AFFECTION.

Charles lay in bed tossing back and forth. He had felt so right about breaking up with Annie. So why was he laying awake for the tenth night in a row?

He looked at the woman sleeping next to him. He experienced a faint but persistent feeling of guilt. He had been single for less than two weeks, and here he was, with his second pick-up of the weekend. It was wrong. Everything was wrong.

Charles made a decision. He grabbed the phone and dialed a car service. When they answered, he shook the girl awake.

"It's for you," Charles said, handing her the phone.

Once she was gone he quickly dressed and combed his thinning hair.

He was really going to do it. He would make amends and apologize.

With every step towards the old neighborhood, he became more and more elated. Sure, he and Annie had needed a break to clear the air. But now everything was going to be fine. After all, they had been living together for six years. They had a cat together.

Charles fiddled with the flowers as he ran up to the doorway. He opened the door. Rushed up the stairs. Rang the bell.

He could see the light go on behind the peep hole. That was quick, Charles thought. Annie must have been laying awake, thinking of him.

The door opened. A curly-haired man with three-day stubble was standing in front of Charles.

"Who the hell are you, knocking on the door at this time of the night?" the man asked.

"Uh . . . who are you?" Charles answered.

"What do you want?" the man said.

"I've made a mistake. I'm sorry," Charles said.

The door slammed shut. Charles was confused. Was he on the wrong floor? Then he saw the shining, new plate on the door: "Welcome to Annie and Gordon's happy home."

Charles sat on the stairs.

Slowly and methodically, he began to eat the flowers. It occurred to him that he didn't know if tulips were poisonous. One could always hope.

Equality Coma

THE COMATOSE CONDITION THAT OVERTAKES BOTH PARTIES IN A RELATIONSHIP WHEN THE PRINCIPLE OF EQUALITY IN THE RELATIONSHIP HAS ECLIPSED ALL OTHER CONCERNS.

The waiter came with the check. Scott started to sweat. He licked his lips nervously. "Darling, this time I'll take the check," he ventured.

"Out of the question," Julie objected.

"Please, I want to treat you tonight."

"Never."

Julie got that stubborn line around her mouth that she only got when she was really annoyed. Like that time when Scott changed the snow tires on the car without asking her to help him. Or when he refused to accept money from her for the new TV set he had bought as a Christmas present for both of them.

"Just because you want to be so manly and not split the check does not mean that my esteem as a woman has ceased to matter. I'm not eating on anybody's charity," Julie hissed.

"It's not about money," Scott said.

"Oh, yeah? That's easy for you to say, you who belong to the sex that for generations has had control over the monetary resources of power."

"Please . . ."

"Give it to me."

Julie snatched the check out of Scott's hands. He looked down at the table. His ears had suddenly turned a deep shade of red.

"Today I pay," Julie said decisively.

"In what way would that be more equal?" Scott asked.

"I make more money, so it's more fair."

"That's the stupidest thing I ever heard. We will split this check."

"In that case we'll split it in proportion to our salaries," Julie said.

"With taxes taken into account," Scott said.

Julie began dissecting the items on the check. Scott looked in his wallet for his last pay stub. Suddenly someone was looming over them, clearing his throat: the waiter.

"I have a message from the manager. He says it's on the house."

"Never," Scott said.

"That's ridiculous," Julie said.

"If it makes you feel any better, it's actually your treat in a way. As soon as you came in we took bets in the kitchen on who would pay the check. The boss won."

Ex-Partner Nausea

SEVERE PHYSICAL DISTURBANCES DUE TO SUPPRESSED ANGER DURING SOCIAL INTERCOURSE WITH YOUR PARTNER'S FORMER BEDFELLOWS.

The party was a great success. John had a great time. Louise was more beautiful than ever, all their friends were there, and the food had turned out wonderfully. A better celebration of their first anniversary would be hard to imagine.

That's when Robert showed up.

Louise met him at the door and hugged him. John's stomach started hurting so bad that he thought that he might throw up. He made a disgusted face, and went out on the balcony and lit a cigarette.

"There you are, honey!" Louise exclaimed. "You have to say hello to Robert, my ex. I don't think you two have met."

"You forget that we were in the same German class in high school," John muttered in a flat voice.

"Oh, I forgot. Isn't that a funny coincidence? But now you guys have to do without me. I have to go and mix some more daiquiris." Louise returned inside, giggling.

John was feeling queasy. He stared at the slimy creep in front of him. The guy was even holding out his hand. John thought he would faint.

"Hi, you can call me Rob."

"Nice to see you again. It's been a long time. Louise has told me so much about you," John said with a wide smile.

"Oh, she did? Well, we had a couple of wonderful years together," the asshole sighed.

"Excuse me. I have to go to the bathroom."

John went inside and sat on the couch in the living room. A minute or two later, the pig appeared again.

"It's such a coincidence," he said.

"What is?" John asked.

"That you and Louise would end up together. How funny."

"Yes, what a funny coincidence." John laughed so loudly and for such a long time that he was close to suffocating when the contents of his stomach came rushing up through his throat.

"How funny that you and Louise would end up together."

"Die a painful death."

Fertility Tolerance

WHEN A POTENTIAL PARTNER'S FLAWS FADE AWAY TO THE SOUND OF THE TICKING OF A BIOLOGICAL CLOCK.

Laura, Theresa and Angie had just begun another round. They were celebrating their ninetieth birthday. They all had all just turned thirty. As always, Theresa was the first to get tipsy.

"Check out that hunk at the bar. I'm going to go and buy him a drink," she said, slurring her words slightly.

Angie smiled. Laura shook her head. Five minutes later, Theresa came back.

"What a jerk," she said. "He suggested we go and have sex against a tree in the park."

"That's disgusting!" Laura said.

"Tell me about it," Theresa answered. "I suggested that we go to his place instead, but he wasn't interested."

After the next round, they all agreed it was Angie's turn. She had been checking out a good-looking guy who was standing at the bar with his friends.

"Haven't we met before?" Angie asked.

"Don't even try it, lady. I won't screw without a rubber," the guy answered.

He and his friends let out one loud, collective laugh. Humiliated, Angie returned to her girlfriends.

"You should have known that might happen," Laura said.

Angie was mad.

"You think you're such a princess just because you have a man at home," she said. "Isn't it about time you dump him, anyway? He's ugly, stupid and has no money."

"But he wants me," Laura answered caustically. "And he wants kids."

The silence was intense. Triumphantly, Laura put two twenty dollar bills on the table, picked up her cigarettes and left.

"What a bitch," Theresa said, slurring her words.

"Shut up," Angie said. "You're drunk." She stood up, threw some money on the table and left.

Theresa was left alone, sitting by herself in snakeskin pants and a low-cut top that showed off her cleavage. She decided to put the moves on a guy dressed in dark clothes who was sitting in the corner. Her vision was so blurred that she couldn't quite distinguish his features, but she thought she saw a mustache on his face.

So it ought to be a man at least.

The Gentility Paradox

THE MAN OF HER DREAMS IS SENSITIVE . . . BUT ONLY IN HER IMAGINATION.

Alone again. Philip looked out through the window of the bar, watching the people milling about on Bleecker Street. Happy people. How little time had passed since he had been one of them.

Three weeks ago, Monica had kicked him out without an explanation. Since then, Philip had been deeply depressed. What had he done wrong?

He had made her breakfast in bed every Saturday morning. Cleaned the apartment. Organized a schedule for their meals throughout the week. Talked about feelings. Only had sex on Monica's initiative. Washed the dishes. Watched "Friends." Always put the lid down after using the toilet. Everything.

Philip heard a familiar laugh and turned around. Monica was standing fifteen feet behind him. Next to her stood a steroid bull with a crew cut, white T-shirt and black jeans. He had one arm around Monica's shoulders and a hand on her ass. Philip felt his stomach seize up.

"I need some booze," the bull said, panting.

"You're such a pig," Monica giggled and squeezed his crotch before scampering off to the bar.

Philip just stood there, staring like a fool. He wanted to throw up, but didn't—out of consideration for the staff. Then the beefcake saw that someone was looking at him. He shouted across the room, "What the fuck are you staring at, you faggot?"

Philip turned around and tried to become as small as possible. He felt his temples pounding. What was Monica doing with this Neanderthal man? Then he felt a heavy hand on his back.

"You piece of shit. You answer when I talk to you, you hear?"

It was the bull. Philip turned on his most sarcastic, nonchalant smile and answered:

"Homosexual, me? Of course, it's my belief that we all are a little bit bisexual, but the fact of the matter is that I lived for three years with the woman you came in here with."

Darkness. Pain. Philip discerned a blurry shape leaning over him as he slowly regained consciousness. It was Monica. She was crying. A smile appeared on Philip's smashed lips. She was coming back to him!

Hairstyle Changing Reflex

THE ABILITY TO TRANSFORM EMOTIONAL PROBLEMS INTO BOUNCIN' AND BEHAVIN' HAIR.

Monica let out a loud sigh. There was nothing in her closet to wear. The red dress she bought last week wouldn't work. Back then, she had had black hair, now it was red. Catastrophe.

The phone rang. It was Lisa.

"You want to go out tonight?" she asked.

"I don't think so. It'll just be bad music and watered down drinks."

"What are you talking about? You always have fun when we go to Bowery Bar."

"I'm tired of that place. I'm thinking about quitting drinking."

"What?"

"I don't like drinking . . . And I have to rearrange the furniture. The apartment looks like hell."

"But didn't you redo the whole apartment last weekend?"

"Exactly. That's when everything ended up in the wrong place."

"Talk to you later."

"Sure."

Monica hung up. Damn, what an ugly phone she had. It was from Radio Shack. The most boring standard model. She had to remember to buy a new one as soon as possible.

She went to the kitchen and opened the fridge. Sausages, ham and three pork chops. Monica wanted to throw up. How could anyone eat meat? From now on, she would be a vegetarian.

"Hello? Anybody home?" Carl called from the door.

"There you are. Did you buy all this crap?" Monica asked, motioning towards the fridge with her hand.

"Um . . . I've missed you too, honey."

"Just answer me."

"You told me you wanted to eat more protein. You said you needed it for that new training program you started yesterday. Monica, is there something you want to talk about?"

Carl put his arm around her. She immediately shook it off.

"I don't have time. I have to dye my eyebrows."

Carl didn't say anything. He had already packed. He had decided to do it when Monica had come out of the bathroom with her hair red again for the hundredth time. He put the keys on the table and left.

Ideal Mate Withdrawal

THE WITHDRAWAL EXPERIENCED WHEN ONE REALIZES THAT THE PERSON ONE FELL IN LOVE WITH HAS ENTIRELY DISAPPEARED.

Patrick wasn't home ýet. Lisa went to the bedroom. The bed was unmade. Next to it: a pile of dirty laundry. A few used condoms littered the floor, exactly where they had landed a week earlier.

Lisa went to the kitchen and opened the fridge. She was thirsty. The fridge was empty, except for an opened can of beer. Patrick had always had such a well-stocked fridge when they first started going out.

Lisa remembered all the wonderful dinners he had cooked for her. Grilled lamb, beef Bourgogne, and bouillabaisse. He couldn't stop telling her about all of the wonderful dishes he made and how popular he had been with his home economics teacher.

Lisa went to the pantry. There had to be something to drink somewhere in the house—preferably of the stiff variety. There wasn't.

Patrick always used to have no less than two cases of good wine on hand. How impressed she had been that time when he taught her how to taste wine. He had explained to her how to detect fruitiness, sweetness and earthy character.

Of course, it was a little embarrassing when he had to sniff, gurgle and spit in the glass every time they ordered wine at a restaurant. On the other hand, that was a while ago.

"Hi darling, I'm home!" Patrick slammed the apartment door. He went straight to the bathroom and peed with the door open. The splashing sound could be heard in the kitchen. Lisa found it nauseating.

"You promised to fix me a nice dinner tonight. Do you remember?" she called.

"Of course," he answered.

"But the fridge is absolutely empty . . ."

Patrick flushed the toilet. He came toward her with a smile.

"Let's just order pizza again tonight, o.k. darling?"

Lovebird Reverb

THE BUZZING IN ONE'S EARS WHICH PERSISTS FOR SEVERAL HOURS AFTER LISTENING TO THE EMPTY BABBLING OF SOMEONE WHO HAS RECENTLY FALLEN IN LOVE.

Helen and Molly had really been looking forward to this: a night out with the girls. Now, sitting at Bar None with Lisa, a bottle of red wine and three glasses resting on the table, they were each trying to remember why. The air of joviality that they had anticipated was somehow entirely lacking.

But this didn't seem to bother Lisa one bit.

"And Peter, you know, he thinks Woody Allen is great. He knows all Woody Allen's one-liners by heart. That one about the valium and the puck is so hilarious. Do you want to hear it?" she asked.

"I think I can do without it," Helen said.

"I've heard it before," Molly said.

"He says I look just like Audrey Hepburn. Everyday, he buys me a little gift. Sometimes it's only a small container of yogurt, but it's the thought that matters," Lisa said quickly.

"Non-fat yogurt or one of those creamy ones?" Molly asked.

"Tell us more," Helen said quickly.

This was the first time Lisa had come out with them since she had met Peter three months ago. Sure, they enjoyed hearing what she was up to . . . But there are limits.

"Peter says that justice is when all people are allowed to realize their dreams. Isn't that beautiful?" Lisa said.

"Yeah, it really is," Molly said.

"What a profound guy," Helen said.

Not until now did Lisa notice the sarcastic tone that Helen and Molly had been answering her with for hours. She fell silent for a moment, gazing at the floor. But before Molly or Helen could even apologize she looked up and smiled. "You don't think I realize that you're being sarcastic, right? It doesn't matter to me because I know that both of you are just jealous," she said.

"Jealous?" Molly and Helen giggled. "What makes you think that?"

"Peter says so," Lisa answered.

The Military Service Reflex

THE PHENOMENA WHEREBY THE TWO PARTIES IN A RELATION-
SHIP, REGARDLESS OF HOW HORRIBLE IT WAS WHEN THE
RELATIONSHIP WAS GOING ON, ONLY HAVE ROOM FOR COZY
MEMORIES AT THE REUNION.

Linda stared at Mary. What little she had picked up during this cell phone conversation was really some of the worst stuff she had heard in a long time. As soon as Mary hung up, she decided to confront her with it.

"Are you going to see Peter? Have you totally lost your mind?" Linda asked.

"Pooh! Having a cup of coffee together isn't such a big deal," Mary answered.

"A cup of coffee? Have you forgotten all he did to you?"

"Stop it, that was ages ago."

"It's only been two months since he put your phone number in *Hustler*."

"Yes, but that was after we had broken up."

"You mean it was after he had burned your clothes because you happened to catch the eye of the guy in the token booth at the subway station or after he told you that you were a boring nobody that he dated only because of your big breasts?" Linda asked.

"We grew apart."

"Perhaps, but I've never heard of any other guy who cuts off his girl-friend's hair because she doesn't return a video on time."

"But he apologized. He explained that he had been psychologically unstable. You should have been there; he looked like a puppy when he told me about his problems."

"Been there? Have you already seen him?"

"He wore the same suit he was wearing the night we first met. He gave me three red roses . . . We talked all night."

"All *night*?"

"When he left the apartment in the morning, I called in sick. I just lay in bed all day luxuriating in his scent. It brought back memories of one particular bed in a hotel room in Italy when we were . . ."

Linda slowly rose from the table. Mary didn't notice anything. She just continued recounting memories, gazing blindly into the distance.

Linda walked towards home. She was trying to remember if she had any Xanex she could spare for Mary. She had a feeling she was going to need it.

"Wasn't she the one you told me was mentally deranged?"

"What?"

Nostalgia Back Flip

THE TRAGIC FINAL PERIOD IN A RELATIONSHIP WHEN LOVE IS NO LONGER WHAT IT IS BUT WHAT IT WAS.

Jenny was woken up by David caressing her back. Sigh. Not again.

"Can't you leave me alone, darling. I'm not in the mood this month. I have a lot to do at work," she mumbled.

Peter grunted something inaudible and rolled over to the other side of the bed.

"Perhaps you could use some of your extra energy to go and fetch the paper instead," Jenny suggested.

"Bitch," Peter mumbled.

"What did you say?"

"Nothing."

As Peter shambled to the door, Jenny couldn't help noticing those unappetizing love handles that had begun to appear around his waist. And those awful hairs on his back that she had always managed not to see when they first met.

On the way back, Peter peed without closing the door. And Jenny couldn't hear the lid being lowered when he was finished either. As he got back into bed next to her, she felt like throwing up.

Then her eyes wandered over to a picture of Greece in the Travel section.

"Oh, do you remember when we went to Santorini?" she said and cuddled up to Peter's chest.

"The dinners we had . . ." Peter said.

"And the walks at night, along the rim of the volcano," Jenny said.

"And those lovely days on the beach, snorkeling . . ."

Waves of memories washed over them as they lay in bed, blissfully staring at the ceiling.

"Do you remember the first time?" Jenny sighed after a while.

"Mmm," Peter said lovingly.

And silently, to himself, he added: *There sure haven't been too many times since then.*

Some time later, Peter remembered that morning and realized that he should have recognized then and there that it was completely over between them. But as things turned out, it took another three weeks.

The thing was, they had had a second trip to Greece, two weekends in Miami and a sex-filled excursion to the Berkshires to nostalgically process before they could finally be through with the thing.

Original Sin Panic

A CONSTANT STATE OF ANXIETY SHARED BY BOTH PARTNERS IN A RELATIONSHIP THAT THEY MIGHT BE TURNING INTO THEIR PARENTS. NOTE: THIS SHARED FEAR IS QUITE FREQUENTLY THE ONLY BASIS FOR THE RELATIONSHIP.

Matt sat in his robe reading the "Metro" section of *The New York Times*. Fanny was reading the "Arts and Leisure" section. Suddenly, Matt broke the silence.

"What fascism! Giuliani wants to impose a $2,000 fine on people who don't pick up their dog's shit," he said.

"We ought to be standing outside City Hall right now giving the mayor the finger," Fanny said.

"It's such a sign of our parents' generation still controlling the world," Matt said.

The morning sun continued to shine brightly into Fanny and Matt's small studio in Brooklyn as the couple continued their conversation as if reading from a script.

Later in the afternoon Fanny and Matt were lying in bed having a conversation about nothing in particular when the same familiar subject arose.

"They just sit there on their fat asses. As far as they're concerned they've paid off all their debts and have a huge Land Rover parked in the driveway—why even move," Matt said.

"I know, I know. My parents truly believe that the meaning of life is to go to Florida in the winter and never have to stop playing golf," Fanny said.

"I love you," Matt said.

He flung himself at her, knocking her off the bed and onto the red bean bag that they had bought second hand. If either of them were honest with the other they would have admitted that they found the thing extremely uncomfortable. But the fact of the matter was that, even though they were both in their mid-thirties, they liked the idea of having teenage furniture. They quickly pushed the beanbag out of the way and made wild and passionate love on the floor.

Partner Revisionism

JUST AS THERE WILL ALWAYS BE GAPS IN ANY HISTORY BOOK ACCOUNT OF A GREAT WAR, SO TOO WILL THERE BE GAPS IN ONES PARTNER'S KNOWLEDGE OF ONE'S PAST RELATIONSHIPS.

Josh couldn't help laughing out loud. What a funny character. Long, curly, blond, poodle-like hair, a studded bracelet, a black leather vest laced up only just above the belly button. And to top it all off, on the shoulder a tattoo which read: "Black Sabbath rules."

"Who is this guy?" Josh called.

"What?" Cynthia called from the kitchen.

"There's this weird guy in one of your old photo albums," Josh said.

"Dinner is ready. Come in to the kitchen," Cynthia said.

Josh gave the tacky rocker a last glance. Cowboy boots. A necklace with skulls. Christ! He put down the album and shuffled into the kitchen.

"It's strange how quickly time passes," Josh said.

"Yes, isn't it? Just a moment ago I put in the pasta and now it's cooked!" Cynthia said.

"It's ironic how incredibly feminine fashions come to be considered so masculine? When you look back, all those rockers from the eighties look like drag queens," Josh said.

"Mmm. The garlic was the perfect touch," Cynthia said.

Later that night, Josh took out the photo album again. But what is this? The pages that had been covered with Mr. Rocker were empty. Strange.

Carrying the album under his arm, Josh went to the bedroom. But he stopped in his tracks at the threshold. Damn! What is she doing?

Cynthia sat cross-legged on the bed. On her lap, she had the small, green cardboard box that Josh kept his diaries in. She had pulled the box out of its secret hiding place in the closet.

She picked up a small, black notebook and fiddled with it, absent-mindedly. "High school, third semester," was written on the cover. Josh could feel his cheeks growing hot and red.

"What a cute little book. I think I'll have a little peek inside," Cynthia said.

"Uh . . . We haven't been to the movies in a long time."

Pizza Incubator

THE FEELINGS OF CONFIDENCE AND TRUST THAT DEVELOP BETWEEN A BACHELOR AND HIS PRIMARY FAST FOOD DELIVERER.

Brad awoke with a headache. He reached out for the Coors Lite on the floor by his bed and knocked it over. Hell. He felt something under his head. It was a note. "You are a large swine. If you ever try to contact me again, I'll give my inheritance to the Hell's Angels in exchange for breaking every bone in your body. Lisa."

What was this? Brad tried to remember last night. Impossible.

He dug around under the sheets for his underwear. They had been cut to pieces. His pants too. And the shirt.

Brad pushed the button on the answering machine.

"Where are you? I've been sitting at Café Fez for hours. This was your last chance. I really hate your guts." Oh. Molly. Beep. "This is Blockbuster. If you don't return the movies tonight, we will initiate legal proceedings." What movies? Beep. "Brad, this is your employer. You'd better get your ass over here right away. There's $800 missing from the register."

Brad pressed stop. He would skip the remaining seven messages. He pressed the first pre-programmed number on the phone.

"Alonzo's pizza."

"Hi. I'd like a delivery please. A medium pepperoni and a coke."

"Hi, Brad. Ten minutes."

Great guy. Always the same answer. Brad took a shower. The buzzer rang just as he pulled on his sweat pants.

"Hi, Brad. That's eight-fifty."

The same old familiar delivery guy.

"Great." He opened his wallet.

Gee. It was empty. He stared at the delivery guy.

"It's okay," he said. "I'll tell Alonzo you'll drop by and pay it tomorrow."

"Are you sure?"

"No problem."

Brad felt a tear forming in the corner of one eye. This was just too much. He searched for words. "Thank you," was all he could manage.

The delivery guy was already hurrying down the stairs.

In this moment Brad decided to invest only in those relationships that really meant something. Women come and go. The pizza man remains.

The Pumping-Up Differential

THE BASIC PRINCIPAL WHEREBY THE MOMENT THAT ONE PARTY IN A RELATIONSHIP (USUALLY THE MALE ONE) IS QUITE CERTAIN THAT HE HAS COMPLIMENTED THE OTHER (USUALLY FEMALE) PARTY IN THE RELATIONSHIP ON ABSOLUTELY ALL OF HER POSITIVE TRAITS, THE OTHER (USUALLY FEMALE) PARTY HAS JUST COMPLETED A LIST OF 100 OTHER ITEMS HE'S FORGOTTEN TO MENTION.

Veronica rose well before the sun that Saturday morning. Jim barely stirred from his slumber as she crept around the bedroom gathering up their laundry. On her way out of the room, arms loaded with dirty clothes, mostly his, she grabbed a needle and thread and her special red dress. Jim—not exactly an elegant dancer—had ripped the hem of the dress with his shoe while attempting to dip her at his cousin's wedding.

And so, she sat in the basement of their building, watching as the wash spun round, carefully re-stitching her favorite dress. When that was finished she made a list of all the items she had to pick up at the grocery store. Veronica returned to their apartment, only to be greeted by a note of—even for Jim—unmatched brevity stating "Gone to Kevin's. Be back later."

At 10:30 that evening Veronica found herself staring at a blackened cornish hen. Kevin hadn't bothered to phone and say he would be late for dinner. Suddenly, she heard a key in the lock.

Kevin found her slouched at the dining room table "I'm so lucky," he began,

with the best of intentions, "how many other guys have a wife so thoughtful she'd have dinner ready for him after the game?" He smiled, apparently not discerning the frown on Veronica's face. "And look at that dress! You look absolutely lovely, honey."

Suddenly Kevin had a brilliant idea.

"This is great, but I'm not really that hungry." He winked at her, a feeble attempt at enticement, "Besides, that dress . . ."

He stood and slowly walked toward her, lightly grabbing her arm to direct her toward the bedroom. Sighing, she reluctantly acquiesced. Trailing behind Jim, she watched as his sneakers dragged mud onto the carpet. In the bedroom, he dove carelessly onto their heretofore tidy bed. She sat hesitantly next to him as he placed his hand between her legs. Veronica gently rebuffed him, instructing him by way of a soft shove to lean back. She moved around and unzipped his pants, moving in closer, mouth wide, teeth ready to chomp down hard.

Radar Malfunction

WHEN THE DESIRE TO MEET SOMEONE HAS RESULTED IN AN INABILITY TO DISCERN THAT ONE SHOULD ACTUALLY TURN AROUND AND RUN.

Linda and Sophie sat at the bar, watching. They had a perfect view of the entire fishbowl. There were twenty-three male specimens in the place. Five of them were over forty. Two had mustaches. Eight were already taken. One had brunette hair with bleached white chunks. One was wearing a pale yellow sweater. Two were gay. And one had a Mickey Mouse tie on.

"It's hard to see that guy in the corner from here," Linda said.

"He's our last hope. I'll go to the rest rooms so I can get a closer look at him."

Sophie came back. Linda leaned against the counter and listened to the report being delivered into her ear.

"Tall, greasy hair, pimples, flannel shirt and cowboy boots," Sophie whispered.

"Did you say tall?" Linda asked.

"Pull yourself together, will you," Sophie hissed.

They sighed heavily and ordered a round of tequilas. Large ones. They quickly downed them and ordered another round.

"Howdy, girls. You look like you haven't had any dick in a long time"

Sophie looked up. One of the mustached guys. What a jerk.

"Is it that obvious," Linda giggled.

Sophie almost choked on her lemon wedge. Oh, my God. Linda had really lost it. How many tequilas had she actually had?

Half an hour later, Linda staggered towards the door with one arm around the neck of one of the mustached guys. Sophie ordered another tequila.

"My God, what a monster. Why didn't you stop me?" Linda screamed on the phone the next morning.

"Oh, so you're still alive?" Sophie said.

"I woke up in a trailer in Atlantic City. First thing this morning he asked if I wanted to be his Eva Braun."

"Congratulations."

"God, you're bitchy. Are you jealous, or what?"

"That's the most ridiculous thing I ever heard. Why would I be?" Sophie said. And hung up.

She sat down on the edge of the bed and rested her hungover head in her hands. Then her eyes caught the pink Mickey Mouse tie on the floor. She took out a pair of scissors and began to methodically cut it into very small pieces.

The Reproduction Gap

THE VIRTUAL ABYSS THAT SEPARATES THE GOALS AND AMBITIONS PEOPLE HAVE BEFORE AND AFTER THEY START HAVING CHILDREN.

Johnny and Laura were stunned when Peter and Julia dropped the Big News. A baby. In just a few months.

"And we have already found the house of our dreams in Maplewood, New Jersey," Peter said with a blissful smile.

"Isn't that a contradiction in terms?" Johnny muttered.

"Our personal bank representative was able to offer us a thirty-year mortgage with a fixed interest rate. It's a very good deal," Julia went on.

"Thirty years?" Laura asked.

"Dad's going to give us his Volvo station wagon. They really *are* practical," Peter said.

Johnny hid his face in his hands. Laura stared down at the rug.

"Does this mean that our trip to Asia is canceled?" she asked.

"What about the snow board company you and I were going to start?" he asked.

Julia and Peter didn't answer. She was busy scratching Peter's neck. Peter was just sitting there smiling ridiculously. He was caressing Julia's stomach. Suddenly, they were having an involved discussion on possible names for the baby.

Finally they left. Johnny and Laura remained sitting on the couch without saying a word. Ten minutes later, Johnny finally said:

"That wasn't my best friend. That was Mike Brady."

"Did you notice how blissful he was when he mentioned the part about the station wagon?"

"They didn't mention it, but I bet they're even buying mutual funds."

Later on, in bed, Johnny suddenly froze, mid-thrust. What was going on? Laura watched him as he scurried to the bathroom. He came back with a small foil package.

"A rubber? But I'm on the pill," Laura said.

"You can't be too cautious when it comes to things like this," Johnny said, rolling it on.

Routine Upset

THE SURPRISE AND SHOCK THAT A COUPLE EXPERIENCES WHEN THEY TRY TO BREAK OUT OF A FIRMLY ESTABLISHED ROUTINE.

Michael lay awake, staring at the ceiling. They really had something good together, he and Jenny. But some of the excitement was gone. A pizza, *Forrest Gump* on the TV and then . . . the missionary position. Nothing wrong in that. It was just a little . . . ordinary.

He looked at the clock. Four-thirty. Three hours from now, it would start all over again. A bagel with cream cheese, orange juice, coffee, and then the bus to work. Just like every morning for the last four years.

Michael felt a mild discomfort in his belly. He knew he would lay there wide awake until dawn.

"What a bombshell I met Friday night. Big boobs, cute as hell and horny like a rabbit, " Hugh had told him over lunch the other day.

"I scored too. Her name was Suzette, she's from Canada. She was a state champion in body-building. You can imagine what that was like," Tom snickered.

Michael didn't say anything.

He passed a sex shop on his way home after work. Without even thinking about what he was doing he entered. Once he had selected the items he wanted he asked the clerk to put them in a unmarked brown paper bag.

At ten-thirty, Jenny suddenly got out of bed "to take care of something." Meanwhile, Michael reached under the bed for his secret bag. Edible underwear. A really sadistic looking mask. A leather strapy suit with lots of chains. . .what was it called?

He heard Jenny call from the bathroom "I'm coming!" He looked up from where he was sitting at the end of the bed, tightening the last straps, and called, "Just a moment."

Suddenly, Jenny was standing before him in a starched white nurse's uniform. With holes cut out for the breasts and the crotch.

Michael and Jenny stared at each in amazement for a few silent seconds.

"Um, nice uniform," Michael finally managed to say.

"Let's just forget the whole thing, okay?" Jenny said.

"Sure."

The Shooting-Yourself-in-the-Foot Strategy

A TERM FOR THE (USUALLY) MALE HABIT OF COAXING A RELA-
TIONSHIP TO END RATHER THAN BEING THE ONE WHO ACTUALLY
ENDS IT.

Helen couldn't believe her eyes. Mark stood only fifteen feet from her, and he was patting a seventeen year old babe in a black turtleneck on her behind. How dare he? She rushed to the ladies room, sobbing.

"Don't be silly. She's an old neighbor of mine, and we didn't do anything," Mark said the next morning.

Helen stared at the ceiling. She was so upset she wanted to die. First, it was the office party that he returned from three days late. Then, all these trips to Aspen with his friends, even though he had never been particularly fond of skiing. And finally—the age-old sign—lipstick on his collar.

The fact that Mark's friends always called him "the stud" didn't help matters either.

"Don't you love me any more?" Helen asked.

"Christ, you're so paranoid! Just because I'm not home twenty-four seven, you think our relationship is over," Mark sighed.

"I didn't say that. But maybe it should be," Helen sobbed.

"Oh, so it's over? Well, I'm not one bit surprised. You women always call it quits the minute everything is not exactly the way you want it."

Mark jumped out of the bed and took out two packed suitcases from the closet. It took him all of ten minutes to gather everything he owned.

"If I've left anything behind, you can reach me at Rebecca's. Here's her number," he said as he handed her his keys.

Three hours later, Helen still lay dumbfounded in their bed. Pulled out drawers, books knocked to the floor, scattered CDs. Wow. She had really done it. She had finally gotten rid of him. But where was that enormous sense of relief she was supposed to feel?

"You going alone to Club Med?"

"Only for three weeks . . ."

Trophy Tenderness

THE PARTICULAR FORM OF AFFECTION THAT ONE FEELS FOR THEIR PARTNER WHEN ONE JUDGES THEM WITH THE SAME APPRAISING EYES THEY USE TO JUDGE A NEW YACHT OR AN EXPRESSO MACHINE.

Alexander couldn't tear his eyes from Yvette. She was standing in front of the mirror in the hall slowly painting her lips a blazing red. They had been together for eight years now. They had absolutely nothing in common and really nothing to say to each other, but the mere sight of her could still take his breath away.

So perfect. So tasteful.

Yvette shook her hair and blew Alexander a kiss before she disappeared out the door. The Jaguar roared in the driveway. Alexander felt incredibly lucky.

Yvette never whined if he had to work until midnight. She got along well with their maid. When they threw parties, she was the perfect hostess. She was hot enough to attract covetous glances from every man in a room. She was also cool enough to make them realize immediately that she was way out of their league and want her still.

"Damn, she has such slender lines," Stuart said as they sat looking at the picture of Alexander's new yacht.

"Wouldn't you just love to be sailing in the Caribbean, drinking a bottle of champagne on her deck right now," Alexander said longingly.

"Perhaps we should take the entire summer to just cruise around on her," Stuart said.

"Mmm, it would be lovely," Alexander sighed.

Stuart poured them another round of single malt whisky. Alexander turned over the vinyl original of Sinatra's "Strangers in the Night."

Yvette had returned from her lover's embrace. She stood outside the window of their study smiling at the two men sitting together fantasizing about god knew what item. She saw Alexander rise and take a few dance steps with an imaginary partner before disappearing out of sight.

He looked so good in a suit. People who say that money can't buy good taste don't know what they are talking about. A better mannequin to bring to her publishing dinners would be hard to imagine. Yes, as long as he didn't open his mouth, he was a great social asset.

Sure, he was worthless in bed, but since he worked so much, he usually fell asleep the moment he hit the sheets, so it wasn't a big problem.

Men are like cars, she thought. First you get one that can give you status and comfort. And then you get another one.

"God, she really is beautiful."

"A nice rear and the loading capacity is okay, but the steering-gear is only so-so."

TTH (Trying Too Hard)

THE TENDENCY TO EXAGGERATE ONE'S OWN IMPRESSIVENESS ON THE FIRST DATE TO SUCH A DEGREE THAT THE OTHER PARTY IS SIMPLY TERRIFIED.

Josh had prepared meticulously. A three-course dinner. Two different wines, champagne with the dessert. Sinatra CDs. He was dressed in a gray, slim-cut Armani suit with a Hugo Boss shirt, no tie. He had left the two top buttons open—so he would look a little casual.

He had taken the day off from work to clean his apartment. In fact, his floors were so clean you could deliver a baby on them. And he was just as clean himself. He had taken such a long, hot bath that, three hours later, his entire body was still red.

He couldn't fail.

"You are so beautiful when you smile," Josh said a few hours later to Karen as they sat on the balcony, eating French cheeses and watching the sunset.

"Your eyes are as deep as all the oceans of the world combined," he said to her as he showed her his leather-bound volumes of Shakespeare.

"Can't we go to my cottage some weekend and pick apples?" he whispered as he lit a fire in the fireplace.

"Surely Monet was a greater artist than Gauguin. Don't you agree?" he asked as he walked over to the Bang & Olufsen stereo he had leased and put on another Sinatra CD.

Suddenly he realized that he hadn't heard a word out of his date in quite some time. When he turned to look at her he realized she was no longer in the room. Josh ran out into the stairwell.

"Karen, come back!" he shouted. But it was too late. He heard the front door to his apartment building slam three stories below.

He felt a wave of depression as he sat down on his black leather Eames chair. He rested his head against his palms.

"What did I do wrong?" he said out loud to the empty living room. Perhaps he should have gotten that puppy after all. Chicks are supposed to fall for that.

Will Vacuum

THE EVENTUAL INABILITY TO MAKE AN INDEPENDENT DECISION THAT AFFLICTS MANY HAPPY, WELL-ADJUSTED COUPLES.

Deborah and Lynn sat on the bus on their way home from work. Lynn pointed at a poster on a passing wall.

"Are you and Rob going to that Star Trek convention this weekend?"

"Oh . . . I hadn't heard about it."

"Wasn't Rob a real Trekkie when you guys met?"

"Yeah, sure, but he hasn't said anything about the convention."

"Of course not. He probably thought you would think that it was too silly."

"Well, I sort of do but. . ."

"Just imagine how happy he'd be if the two of you went... for his sake."

Deborah ruminated over what Lynn had said on her walk home from the bus terminal. She couldn't think of anything dorkier than being obsessed with Star Trek. She had almost told Rob that the first time they met. She had never had to say anything. Over time Rob had realized that she wasn't "one of them."

But what if Lynn was right? Perhaps he watched tapes of Star Trek when she was out. Or pretended he was Captain Kirk and she one of those women-from-another-planet when they were having sex.

"Darling, I thought we could go to that Star Trek convention Saturday," Deborah said when she and Rob were sitting in front of the TV set that night.

"Do you want to?"

"If you want to."

"Well, if you like. . ."

The next morning, they stood in a line of people one hundred yards long. They were the only two bored people in the line. Everyone else was busy reciting different episodes of Star Trek and then listening to someone else recite another episode back to them. When they got to the door, the cover charge was twenty dollars. Per head. Deborah tried to hide her wry face as she paid.

"What's wrong?" Rob asked once they were inside.

"Nothing."

"Don't you want to go?"

"I don't care. I'm going for your sake."

"What? I'm here only because you wanted to go."

"Didn't you want to go?"

"Of course not. I outgrew Star Trek a long time ago."

The asshole at the door refused to refund their tickets. On their way out Deborah was knocked over by a Dr. Spock.

Index